classic rough news

KENNETH FIELDS

THE UNIVERSITY OF CHICAGO PRESS
Chicago and London

KENNETH FIELDS is professor of English and creative writing at
Stanford University.

The University of Chicago Press, Chicago 60637
The University of Chicago Press, Ltd., London
© 2005 by The University of Chicago
All rights reserved. Published 2005
Printed in the United States of America

14 13 12 11 10 09 08 07 06 05   1 2 3 4 5

ISBN: 0-226-24860-7 (cloth)
ISBN: 0-226-24861-5 (paper)

Library of Congress Cataloging-in-Publication Data

Fields, Kenneth, 1939–
    Classic rough news / Kenneth Fields.
      p.   cm. — (Phoenix poets)
    ISBN 0-226-24860-7 (cloth : alk. paper)
    ISBN 0-226-24861-5 (pbk. : alk. paper)
      I. Title. II. Series.
    PS3556.142C58 2005
    811'.54—dc22

                                    2004005366

For Nora Cain
who knew before I could know

A poet, if he aspire to write the true Classic Rough Newes, must be Scholarly, Scattered, & Mad.

— JEREMY FICKLE,
A Treatise on the Phantastikal Understanding (1763)

I have drunk, and seen the spider.

— WILLIAM SHAKESPEARE,
The Winter's Tale

Contents

Acknowledgments

My thanks to the publications where the following poems have appeared:

Chicago Review: "Separate Camp," "In the Wain," "Going Out," "Realizations,"
  "The Last Infirmity," "The Passive Voice," "Opening Line," "Arkansas
  Stone Medium," "A Short History"
Persea 3: An International Review (1983): "On the Bus," "Fair Nice Pieces, or
  Burton Makes His Move," "Here Nor There," "On the Verge,"
  "In the Name of the Queen," "Royal Burton," "The Narrow Road
  to the North"
Sequoia: "The Company," "And Company Kept," "Powerhouse," "No Moon
  at All"
TriQuarterly: "The Rules of the Game"
Uncommon Touch: Fiction and Poetry from the Stanford Writing Program: "The
  Rules of the Game," "La Salamandre," "Opening Line"
Writers' Forum: "In the Place of Stories," "Tangled," "Imprisoned Lover
  Singing Freedom," "Apology," "La Salamandre"

CLASSIC ROUGH NEWS

Separate Camp

The scattered books on my side of the bed,
Torn covers, broken backs, and the hacked limbs—
A fortress in defeat, or under siege,
At best a losing battle. Will my life,
Clutters, dustrats, middens of papers, gradually
Topple in visions that would kill a wino?—
Dishearten the purest nun? Is this my France,
Hyperdefended, my old Maginot Line?
A cluttered, like a cloistered virtue squints,
Missing the closest foe: castle and host,
Book and bookworm, clap and claphound. I know
Myself what I fear the most. Priesthoods of self,
Cutting my nose or something worse to spite
The unexorcised adversary of my life.

In the Place of Stories

You tend to lose yourself here, friend. Come in . . .
Come in to the dark, come in to the music playing,
Come in to not knowing who you may become.
Here in this bar, The Nut House, you hear the titles
Of a thousand stories, the head is dizzy with them—
A whole life latent in a little line—
Broken off by the cash register, the click of balls,
A nearmiss score, another record. "Hell,
I've been cheating on her since our divorce."
"Ain't there a family man in this fucking place?"
"Don't play me for a sap"—each wounded cry
Gone as soon as said, teasing out of us
Incomparable ghosts—"I said I was a fairy, man,
Not a magician." You see what I mean.

In the Wain

No wine today, only its ghost. Goodbyes
Are sadly easier than I'd imagined.
Just when my teeth were fixed—those broken dreams
Of losing it, those craters now more secure
Than money in the bank, with enough gold to send
My cunning driller off to Cabo San Lucas
Whirring his Margaritas; just when my doctor
Told me I was just fine . . . "except you should
Go on the wagon a couple of months, retest
To see if you should ride it all the way out
To the end of the line—at least you'll get the full trip!"
Born under the dark winestar, Burton assures us
The melancholy man laughs last,
Not necessarily, no, not necessarily best.

Along the Watchtower

"Mixing with the world is clarifying," thought
Montaigne, who found us much confined, pent up—
Fearing experience as if it were the plague—
Seeing our noses clearly, or a little more,
Perhaps the black on white beneath the walls,
Disdainful of the clamor beyond the moat.
Montaigne, the irrepressible, leaps up
Clean from the page—who'd want to keep *him* out?
Still there are others who require some losses
Before we can entertain them. Stiffening, we
Forget that "when reason fails us we make use
Of blessed experience." Aren't we too much like
"Men squaring the circle, lying upon their wives?"—
Locking the barndoor before the horse gets in?

The Last Infirmity

"Fame is a motherfucker!" the poet saith.
Or was it a spur, or a two-handed engine?
Whatever that means. Anyhow, it seems,
From this blue side of the great divide,
Sometimes a well, more often a poisoned spring
In the mankilling, twenty-mule borax flats—
The pointing finger, not the moon. The astronauts,
Their womb was galaxies, had to come down
At last to a stifling, uncaring world,
Shrink-bait forever. The new law, or the old?
It doesn't matter. Outlaws themselves, the judges
Hang sharpies, snake oil salesmen, drifters, and whores
And love their work! O that mirage, that courthouse,
I dream of the drinking fountain beside the door.

The Daily Mirror

I'm apprehensive, going to see my shrink
For the first time ever, and me a greenhorn,
And at my age, and without a drink! No fault,
The best policy I can hope for now. Alas,
My faults are heavy on me, and at my age
So much the fabric, neither warp nor woof—
So much the tree, what can I do but bark?
I have no great manic thirsts, just little mundane ones
Here and there, while I watch myself. The music
From here on out in black and white is Bartok—
Atonal, strident, not yet my cup of tea—
With no bar but the terrible, binding one
Quavering with decision till closing time.

The Art of Surprise

Robert on acid, Robert on down the line,
Robert on Southern Comfort, Robert on joy!
The old folks say the old days never come back.
Well, that's what makes 'em old. What makes 'em new?
Little things, mostly. Stuck in with the bills,
A cashier's check from John Beresford Tipton
(Which dates us both) and all tax free. Patience,
Hard thing, a million! For all the rest,
Long days of disappointments, our preparations
Telling us *take ahold, own up*: "I, Robert Weston,
Once made this little haiku of surprise,
Running a moonshine road to the unforeseen:
'The sleeping bag,

                     rolled up at the foot of the bed—
        Look!
                  the cat
                         is pissing on it!'"

Eyewhite Nightlight

The little mouths of poppies—ah, what a blast!
The initial liftoff of the rocket, bound
For the darkened, edgy goddess of clear air,
"Medallion of insomnia, or Endymion."
Classically spare or, waxing, radiant
With someone else's fire, she is a sign
Scored by our need for freedom at any cost
Over the door of nothing. Her devotion,
Thin as a knifeblade, needs but the thinnest wafer.
That scrap of shredded paper in your wallet,
The number scrawled in a stranger's hand, will do,
If anything will, for your ticket. Overhead,
You turn your white, scarred face through the noxious air
To the tiny pale white flowerlets of our pain.

The Company

Classes, "up in the morning and off to school,"
The only part worth dying for. But the meetings!
A sort of Dugway Utah Proving Grounds,
Test flights for deanhood—the right stuff, chicken colonels,
"The heart of the university." And the students?
Listen, we let them go to meetings, too,
Previews of coming attractions. The difference
From fledgling to cluck, only about sixty thousand—
Kernels to scratch the pen for, unlike the range
Of the grads of the GSB (not GBS),
A million clams at high tide. So we scratch,
And snatch, and peck, getting our strokes somehow.
But let that pressured blood show, just a drop
Staining the eye or feathers, and the cocks and hens,
Knowing a *symbol* when they see one, will
Deconstruct that sucker down to ammonia.

And Company Kept

But what of those mornings when we used to walk,
Head down, heel to toe, the new shoes
Truly appreciated every step of the way?
What of our fuddled days eager to learn
Or eager, at least, to be where the learning was?
Timmy always the conductor, I always played the clogs—
Which, girls, is like singing alto, "altos, come in":
Dah dah dah, which sounded like nothing then,
But is the choir of learning, faint nowadays
Over the noise of the grinders. "Let us be,"
It seems to say, "as little children, once again
Engrossed in what we do."
                              "Can I come home with you?
. . . Tell your mama and your papa, O
Yeah—I'm a little school boy, too!"

Going Out

Billie was nervous, she had to be. . . . To *be*—
What with all the risks, and the faint heart
Sometimes out of control and sometimes stopped—
That gave her a fright, all right. Besides,
Seeing that virtue is time spent, hadn't she
Done everything that everybody wanted?
Freight trains, lasers, and cancer cells were not—
She knew this most assuredly—any more
Determined than her fierce programmed unswervings.
But the world "at large" like a madman—hadn't they
Failed, at present, to chart it all?   At the door
Looking into herself, she saw them vanish—
The disease, the sharply directed, the scheduled run—
And looking, saw little else. She tried the bell.

Realizations

Wonder of wonders, new heaven and new earth!
And she was in it now . . . she didn't know
How, or exactly how. Her situation
Was questioning her, to say the least. At least,
Feeling herself, she wasn't someone else,
She didn't think so. . . . Not since yesterday—
When her brain seemed like numberless galaxies,
Her feet the endlessly rocking—had she flinched
Before the vertiginous gulf of latencies.
Now that she asked, she knew she felt murderous—
Who wouldn't? Didn't the others feel it, too?
Did self-respect demand of this sharp potential
That she bring it into the light, as blinding steel?
Such candor, Billie had to admit, had a certain appeal.

Imprisoned Lover
Singing Freedom

Chainsaws were comforting to Billy's mind.
Finesse was out of the question. Levelling
Good wood and rotten, noisy, irreversible—
Like Billy at his best—they cleared his head
Like the bars he came to after the killing floor
Of Southeast Asia, where he had prayed for death . . .
The humiliated, he knew, inherit the earth.
Wasn't he the only luckless man he knew
Who, screwing his courage to the sticking point,
Went (scared) to a new massage parlor only to find
Miss Emily didn't do windows! His regular girl,
High spirited, volatile, lived in the cupboard,
Sang *lieder*, each more impassioned, till five o'clock,
Then trembled in the glass beside him all night long.

The Interior Castle

Alone, he heard voices, which was not surprising.
Religion did funny things. Did Billy suppose
That La Pucelle and Teresa and those other ladies
Had done it without booze? He did not suppose.
To each his own, his protestant, mystic rule.
And yet he felt hidden from his hidden god,
But did his bidding, loved his narrow cell,
Suffered the lash of inwit, yes, and fasted
To be a worthier vessel for the spirit's light.
In time the voices grew, he came to feel
Somewhat reluctantly, into his own:
"This is my blood, the spirit that hates the world,
Take it, and drink." He prayed in his unbelief,
Then took his humiliation like the cure.

On the Bus

With witty, finical care, Burton would cite
Hundreds of texts to prove the scholarly mind
Was most lamentably inclined to melancholy,
Though also to *hilare delirium*:
The madman, say, "with a Bible in his head,"
Or Thomas Aquinas, dining with the king of France,
Suddenly slapping the table, and crying out
"This breaks the Manichaeans!" On the bus
Burton himself had missed a stop or two.
Didn't the plumber take pains to clean his snake,
Especially after the job? the painter, his brushes?
But the thinker, sending his brain faster than greyhounds
Around the world, only sharpened his pencils.
Burton thought they would die when they got the point.

Fair Nice Pieces, or
Burton Makes His Move

The man of sixty turning his thoughts to love
After a life of study has it made,
Burton consoled himself. Hadn't he read
More pieces on love than Casanova had?
Admittedly long in the tooth, but better hung
(He saw the old masters heavy on his walls)
With wisdom than the young, he nevertheless
Faltered a little. "Generally to fair nice pieces
Old age and foul linen are two most odious things . . ."
But young people loved Yeats, and hadn't he
Understood Burton more and more these days?
At last he was ready to put aside his books—
From the decline of the West through Strauss he understood
"The owl of Minerva begins its flight in the dusk."

At the Laundromat

Watching her life go round, Billie recalled
Her former confidante, the only one
To whom she'd been able to display her unmentionables—
Things that she wouldn't even tell her shrink.
She was a friend, she'd guessed (how could you tell?)
And best of all, all ears. Billie poured out
Secrets so close she learned them in the tumbling
Over and over, and Kathy didn't mind,
Not even the midnight calls when intimacy
Became a burden, which Kathy always bore
Till Billie hated her. She hated the eye
Through which she could see the hidden bits of lace
That she permitted herself, tumbling around . . .
She'd never come clean again, not in this place!

Here Nor There

In the East Burton was home, Allah be praised!
He "became" a bedouin, and around the fire
Heard thousands of tales . . . and none with the ignorance
He thought he'd left behind: the young bridegroom
Who found his bride chloroformed in bed,
This note pinned to the pillow: "Mama says
You're to do with me what you like." The violence
Quickening his blood here, delicately spiced
By the manual grip of holy books of love.
Yet sometimes he missed a simpler innocence—
St. Francis, seeing a man and a maid engaged
In a dark corner, lifting up his hands,
"Thank God for this Christian Charity!" It would be years
Before he would write, "The world is growing vile and bête."

The Passive Voice

Ropes had been used, that much was clear. The rest—
The ninety-nine stab wounds and the underwear—
Was lost to the official flatteries of the press:
"The victim was found at 9:18 last night . . ."
Who cared about the minute! "and there was
Evidence of a struggle. The ropes appeared
To be exceedingly tight, and numerous,"
And 'applied with loving care,' somebody said.
"The police suspect foul play." They didn't say
A note had been left,* they never said enough,
Not for the whole picture. And so much more
Might have been said, you know. But the brief account,
As tantalizing as a pink slip of a tongue,
Was eagerly, eagerly seized on by several readers.

*8 5 14 18 9/
11 14 15 23 19/ 4 21 20 3 8/
4 9 4/ 9 20.

On the Verge

The Perfumed Garden, a moslem work of love,
Held ignorance of shared pleasure to be a sin,
Gave hundreds of names for things that barely had
One name where Burton came from: *the crested one*,
With a red comb that rises with full arousal,
The unionist, the crusher! . . . And the verge,
The tailor, swimmer, housebreaker, liberator,
All with such nice distinctions: the *dok el arz*
("This is the veritable manner of making love!")
That favorite with all the ladies, especially
When doing the *tachik el heub*, or "hair to hair."
Somehow Victorian England wasn't game
For the book he hoped might save it. After his death
His wife burned the crown of his life, one page at a time.

A Short History

"Texts" or "signs" or (worse) "traces," it appears,
Projected themselves, not books that people read.
And the author, the fat, bristly doctor, say,
Became an expedient synecdoche, "Dr. Johnson,"
Who didn't write his books—they were just written.
A curious people, they put poison in their food
(And knew it) to make meat redder under glass,
Translated languages they didn't understand,
And looked, for the cures of the plagues that science caused,
To science . . . whose disinterested shamans feared
When they dropped the first Big One that it might
Explode the atmosphere—in which unlucky event
The world would have disappeared. One deconstructionist
("Freeman Dyson") insisted, "The bomb was dropped."
Such passive modesty before such a grand florescence!—
The radiance of a culture *sous-rature*.

In the Name of the Queen

Burton detested all that Her Staidness stood for.
Odd that his partner dreamed of the queen each night,
Confusing her with his mother, begging him back
From the sinewy girls he refused to "domestic bliss
So interesting and beautiful in our English homes."
At home Burton had a wife who also dreamed,
Pleading to The Unamused: "Madam, I shall
Cry like an angel of justice." So Burton carroused,
Fondled, and measured, defining his liberty
As everywhere she was not . . . while unspeakable Speke,
The abstemious prude, upstaged him, and even named
His lake and falls for the goddamned bitch! Two men,
Peas in a pod, two sides of the same medal,
Neither one guessing they were both Victorians.

Royal Burton

Imagine Burton married to Cleopatra,
Around the world in eighty ways or more!
Who could tire of her world? those two soft
Hemispheres touched with violet—"Were these the eyes,"
Burton intoned, "that launched a thousand scripts?"
But was this what he wanted? His golden voice
Bawling for liquor in the afternoon?
They had it all on film. Two quarts a day,
Fighting, eating, and screwing across Mexico,
With iguanas every night, soon added up . . .
Twelve million bucks, and fifty pounds apiece.
And their subjects loved it all. Still laboring under
His dreamy queen, Burton saw in them both
The veritable anatomy of melancholy.

A Country Story

"When I was a little girl back in East Texas,"
My mother's mother, Beulah, used to tell,
"There was an outbreak of the German measles,
Mama was pregnant, so I went away
To a neighbor lady's, three or four miles from home
When the first signs showed. I was just eight, and sick,
And lonesome for Mama. One day she came for me.
My little sister had broken out, and Mama
Figuring she would die, and the baby, too,
Wanted us all together for those last weeks.
She wanted me home with her. As it turned out
My sister had been reading by the fire
And broke out from the heat, and it was me
That carried the measles home. After Mama died
I used to think of seeing her out the window
Talking to the neighbor lady on that day,
Crying and wiping her eyes with her apron hem."

Voices of Silence, or
The Camaraderie of Influence

Our ancestors? Well, family, certainly,
Then families of friends, and books. Ford Madox Ford,
A stretcher of points, saw fiction as a life,
Recalled with deep affection a gentleman
He'd met at a garden party years before,
Counted him as a friend, only to find
Him tucked away in one of the minor tales
Of Henry James, a friend. This sort of thing
Drives wild his scholars, among whom is a friend.
We would do well to love our predecessors
Not anxiously. Others were here before us,
Offering their fellow-feeling. Listen to one
On his ancestors, Sir Thomas Browne: "We mercifully
Preserve their bones, and pisse not upon their ashes."

Apology

Chairmen, deans, provosts, and presidents,
I meant no harm, really! It was all in fun,
We all can work together, I know it now.
Oh sure, I used to bristle, calling you
All sorts of names I wouldn't mention now,
But that was in my salad days. Now I see
The light at the end of the accounting room. Like a pair
Of shoes, we can walk together (though a friend
Wore an unmatched pair for two weeks before he noticed
A pain in the ass). Just think of the great teams:
Nitro & glycerine, water & oil, beer
& ginger ale, Nixon & Robert Lowell.
The other day I saw two blackbirds perched
On the back of a dark horse, waiting for the full coarse
Packets of undigested grain. Enough!
"We have one sap and one root—"
                                        One sap indeed—
Now is the time to share and share alike!

The Narrow Road to the North

Burton looked at his wall, and went to Japan.
Those prints, now loosened, drifted, now filled his room
Like snow, like the daylight moon outside his window—
Remote, yet close enough to touch. He watched two mallards
Grazing a moon no bigger than themselves,
One taking off, the other about to land there,
The flat feet flared and ready. And from a sky
Of whiteness, small flakes were looming, till they became
Three great white snow geese nearing a moony branch . . .
All of them travellers through a floating world
Of seasons, winds, and currents. Which one was he?
The question turned through his mind and he watched it go.
It was enough to be here where he was
So sure of himself for the moment that he didn't care.

"Into the World of Light"

Somewhere along the Beautiful Ohio
A young man, twenty-five, whom I scarcely knew,
Is suddenly taken. This news has shaken me
Here on this sunny, windy, summer day
As if he were a friend, which he surely was.
Why are we taken by these brief encounters,
These glimpses of a life? Is it because
They hint at futures brighter than our own . . .
Than anybody's? . . . now only memories,
And only a few at that? Walt, here's all I have:
That vegetarian pizza (a disaster!),
An afternoon of stories, old photographs,
And guacamole served in (of all things)
A blue ceramic hat! And now, too soon,
This bright day is all yours. May you get through it
In your curious, patient way, and in days ahead
"When our futures, taken from us, are given back"
I pray for your gentleness, to know you better.

Daggers & Patchwork Quilts

Naturally drawn to draperies, darkened interiors,
Or the fading rosiness of dawn and dust—
Pale moods and atmospheres to be waited on—
Burton confessed it, something was left out,
And that something was himself. Over his door
"Tread softly because you tread on my dreams"
Seemed less and less his motto. He longed for the "hard
Sophoclean light," the quirky dagger of style,
And found them both in a pointed sentence of
G. A. E. Parfitt, on Sir Thomas Browne:
"He is a Protestant Bossuet whose panegyrics
And unsubstantiated assertions,
                                backed
By a wealth of erudite references,
                                are conveyed
In the private rhetoric
            of a continually speculative mind."

The Rules of the Game

At first it was better than fun—the companionable nights,
The whiskey by the fire, the dark behind us,
The light inside us lifting the old tales
Over the ancient woods. But even then
The game was receding from our hearts. By now
It has been years since anybody saw
The great brown bear, now even the squirrels and rabbits
Are talking to themselves, and the old forest
Has dwindled to this lawn below the porch
Where I've sat hunting in my peculiar way,
The lights and liver darkening, the last cloud
No bigger than a man's hand, one of my own.
So whistle up the dogs, and piss on the fire,
This was the last hunt, and it's over now.

Powerhouse

Resentment gnawed at Billie like a bone.
She dreamed of power, and had it in her hand
Only at home alone, with the lights turned low,
The family hit list growing in her mind
Till no one was left but her. She mourned for them
Only until the daylight brought them back
Like vampires in reverse. Then the black dogs—
Her boss, her mother, strangers in the street—
Howled at the door, or used the telephone,
All of them out to get her . . . A tiny sun
In a universe of mirrors, she was sure
That everything said to her was about her,
That the moon burned with *her* heat. Like the inverted thief,
His mind a prison cell, she couldn't stand
The thought that everyone everywhere made love without her.

Breathless

Billy demurred—well, inwardly, at least—
That was always his way. In there he was dark,
Low lighting, fog, and a high-angle shot,
The tilted hat, the cigarette, and behind him
The alley of a thousand melodramas,
Killers with heart, and heroes without honor,
He'd watched them in the darkness all his life.
Nobody knew to look at him, five foot four,
Green-eyed and shy, that he was a killer, too,
And knew all about love: "Something between
A man and a .45 that doesn't jam."
Sure, he'd had a few troubles—the moving dolly
Filming his life just wouldn't let him go.
He touched himself to make sure he was all there.

Torch Singer

Besides his steady girl, who never talked
Except through him, Billy tried several others
Who never recognized his boozy song
Or saw the unsteady flickering in his hand.
He whispered out his love in between drinks
Over the phone to women he didn't know . . .
Why were they in the book if they didn't want
His hot breath cutting like electric wire?
This was his secret life. Others might find
His loving odd, they wouldn't understand,
Even with the clues he dropped. Oh, he was careful
With his belladonnas, yet he gave himself away
Oddly, as when he wrote to his two friends,
"Dear Carmen and Ernie: So how's Ernie?"

Early Autumn

It's been three years today, who would have guessed it?
Without a drink and happy! Unobsessed,
The black dogs of resentment worry less
At me, their chief contention, their old bone.
Whoever held me like a glass of wine
Now holds me like a sound I scarcely hear . . .
Whoever brought me down now lifts me up,
Whoever. . . . I am taken by a wind
"From the round earth's imagined corners" now
Into a calm I've never felt before.
It comes and goes. Outside, beneath my window,
Along the pavement, a young bird like a leaf
Flutters toward cover. I pray for the helplessness
Of birds, of cats, of foxes, and of wolves—
All of us in the game!—the hounds of autumn
Testing the air, the summer's fading traces.

Right Now

It's nineteen years today since he last held
A drink in his hand or held his breath while smoke
Filled as much of him as he could stand
Till, letting it out, he sought oblivion
Of the trace of memory or anticipation,
And his life fell into a death spiral. Since then
He's been around folks like him. When he's been asked,
And sometimes, eager, when he hasn't been,
He talks to the ones who are not even sure
They want to learn how to stop killing themselves.
That feeling still seems close to him some days.
Right now he's okay, and that's enough, right now.

Winding Up

Who would have thought Billie would turn to drink?
Her father and mother and sisters were all alkies
And to be one of those things was the sorriest lot
Billie could ever imagine. They'd needed her
And, God, she had served them, waiting hand and foot
On every little whim, then the sonsofbitches
Left her in the lurch and gave up drinking!—well,
Two by dying, but the others went cold turkey . . .
She began to burn, as if they'd laid her off.
Think of it! No more pain, no more attention
Enraged and finicky, no unpredictable
Storms to withstand, she thought, beside the sink
As she twisted the neck off another cold one. Hell,
Here it comes, Sister, somebody had to do it.

No Moon at All

Billy thought everybody knew his secret.
Everybody but him. Oh, it was there,
Burning its hidden delight beyond the dark
Bowl of confining sky. Everyone else
Somehow divined it, even whispered its name
The minute he walked in. He needed a drink
Whenever he met strangers, suspicious agents
Who might, he was afraid, reveal it to him.
He wasn't an alcoholic, that much he knew,
That had been clear for years. But he was afraid
That people might think he was. How could they know
That he needed this much wine to feed the flame
Of the thirsty hidden god within. What was he?
Showing them whatever it was, whoever they were?

Arkansas Stone Medium

Knives were the answer. Billie collected them,
The Gonzo Gerbers and the Family Bucks,
Patton pearl handles, wood, steel, bone, and horn,
And the beautiful blades, the hardened *delicatesse*
That held her in the light. With her pills and wine
She worked them over every night, her friends,
Put them to the stone incessantly; the sound,
Like a sibilance of leaves, *simoon, simoon*,
The prophetic wind of god, gave her a future
As monotonously compelling as solitaire.
A self-fulfilling sibyl, she walked everywhere
With her pockets full of death, and until dawn
She honed herself along the shaping stone,
The thinning edge turned dull from sharpening.

The Bookworm Dreams of
Toughboy Poetry

While the boys who laugh at him are Letting The Good Times Roll,
PB enchants himself into the books
That he has to love and, humming Rip It Up,
He knows he'll be a critic. Toughboy on the page!
Outside, the cherry '40 Fords parade,
Bo Diddley Gunslingers out with Poison Ivy,
But twenty years later, when His Aim Is True,
His monicker, Percy Bysshe, would strike terror in them
(He'd kill those fucks, his parents, for that one, too!)—
He'd have his own prosaic magazine
With poetry that didn't seem like poetry—
They'd snickered at him too long. Well, It's My Party,
And It's Judy's Turn to Cry, The Toughboy Dreams
Of Toughboy Poetry, In The Still Of The Night,
Don't Do No Good To Squeal,
Oh, Tutti Fruiti, Yes, I'm the Great Pretender.

Under the Lamplight

Burton was odd. Burton loved the dentist,
Especially his pretty assistants. Were uniforms
Merely the image of things to be removed,
A glimpse of those undiscovered worlds therein,
"The Sansculottist Sea of Light and Love,"
A Philosophy of Clothes? And the little pain,
His mouth wide open, as they brushed his arm
(His *imprisoned* arm) with their unconscious limbs,
Well, somehow it was meant for him. The probes and scraping,
Burton imagined they made his teeth hard, too!
When the real pain started, he had a trick or two
Picked up in a book he'd forgotten as a boy.
He simply read himself. From above the chair
He watched the odd commotion beneath the lamp.
He thought he made out the title, *The Razor's Edge*.

The Invariable Paths

Sundown again. Since Bobby left, the sky
Left over from dark to dark calls aimlessly,
This is the first drink. The whiskey light,
On its way through fire to the blackout, used to be
Her time, and now without her, it still is.
Her fingers touch her as she sees the street lights,
The invariable veins of love, in the valley below
Come on with their bright traffic. Later, perhaps,
She'll fade out of herself. Perhaps tonight
Billie won't even remember going to bed,
Won't have the dream of the old man selling rabbits,
Won't remember the knife, or the radio
That brings her back each day, that whispers now,
"Maybe tomorrow, I've done enough dying today."

Being of Sound Mind

The will, as it must, thought Burton . . . well, must what?
For years he'd been a cultist of control
With none for himself. Like the astronomer
In *Rasselas*, who thought he governed the sun
And all its appurtenances, Burton believed
And did not see that he willed what already *was*,
The static world without him. Serapion
Could easily have vied with him, "I am deader than you!"
Montaigne believed the penis, against the will
So tirelessly pitted, was framed by our other members
To make us think it was the only one
"Refusing our solicitations both mental and manual,"
While the others rioted anyhow. Dr. Johnson
Spoke of our stubbornness, "A dead man will
Make a coughing sound if they are lifted around,"
At least as Burton recalled it, a dead man will.

Phantom Pain

Billy could never remember Bowen's name,
His best friend in the jungles. Bowen's way out
Was to be dead already, no suspense,
"Ain't no big thang." It was like having a friend
Who wasn't there, who was safe. His other names,
Taxi, for instance, or Mr. Bullethead,
Were on the tip of his tongue, but never Bowen.
He probably didn't notice, was probably elsewhere,
When the bicycle bomb took him, and his favorite bar,
And half a block of Saigon, leaving the name
That Bowen almost was, the whiskey trembling
Above the rim of his shotglass. But Billy noticed—
He couldn't remember, and he couldn't forget . . .
Like the legless figure of his dreams, his mother,
The martyred drinking lady, Catherine.

Among the Mysteries

Edwin Drood. Burton's been reading all day
The mystery of Dickens' final evenings—
English Cathedrals, Sultans, Opium,
The "wittles" the Princess Puffer smoked for hunger:
"I got Heavens-hard drunk for sixteen year afore
I took to this; but this don't hurt me," she said,
"Not to speak of." Burton had seen it before
In Arabia Deserta, in the fabulous harems,
Desire raised to a theory, and on the stagecoach,
With the alkies strapped to their seats, riding for days
Toward the City of the Saints, the Desert Lion,
And the strange visions of abstemiousness,
Labor, and many wives. Thus Brigham Young,
When Burton jokingly asked to be taken in
To the fragrant folds of Zion, laughed, "Captain Burton,
I should think you'd done this kind of thing before!"

Cutting His Losses

Bars were his life. He kept getting thrown out.
"I drinks a bit," Billy would tell his friends
Back when he had them. He never threw things away,
He simply lost them, or he left them behind,
So a little less of him came back each day.
"It'll be safer there," he always said—
A shirt, a knife, a photograph, his name,
A list left in a bar or on the bus.
He drank a bit the morning he walked downtown,
Only two beers on the way to the liquor store,
When the seizures caught him, black suns, bright suns—
He couldn't shake them, couldn't lose these things—
The slap of the sidewalk, the electric yellow faces.
He didn't hear the sirens. He talked to them,
The paramedics, as if they were old friends:
"You guys like things that I don't more than I do—
I can't stop thinking about it."
                                        "What?"
                                                "I can't remember."

Tangled

The rabbits were at the door, a little bulge
Just above the left eye. The rattlesnakes
Tangled above her knees as the bedclothes turned,
"Another transparent night." The songs were singing
Every day now even while she was driving,
Her little finger buzzing like the end of a tail,
Her toos cant moos, this was not being well.
She began to dream of someone who needed her,
Somebody lost on the highway, left
To dry on the line, barbed wire, telephone wire—
The whips and jangles, nothing coming clear,
The buzzing static on the radio,
Heat-seeking, diamondhead,
And safety somewhere beyond those coils of sound.

The Break

He shuffled along the corridors for days,
Shaking against the walls, shutting his eyes
When he passed a doorway or met another patient,
As if a look could burn him to the quick.
He could feel violence in the filtered air.
Mostly the smilers frightened him. At the thought
These people want to love you, Billy fled
Backward and inward down that silent well
From which had arisen his last cry *you don't need this*
Until the waters poured into his mouth,
Went still over his head, what blessedness!
The only one to reach him was Yvonne,
Next-to-the-last cast with After-the-first,
He might have been Yvonne, she didn't ask
Anything of him, she just told him stories,
Her stories of burning up, drinking away
Her life so palpable within him that
One day he laughed out loud at some disaster
Diminished by her getting on with it.

Battle Review

Burton didn't do it, but he knew somebody,
A paragon of will, who held his hand
"With dignity and restraint" over a candle
While the flesh melted; who, as a little boy,
Had eaten a rat to kill his fear of them,
The will and reason lording cowardly feelings,
Knowing the rats would fear him and the cat—
"They both eat *us*," a formalist victory,
All hat and no cattle. "It will never be popular,"
And it makes Seneca look like a Sybarite—
(He was, a friend reminds me)—this discipline,
This time-honored lash. Burton knew an Irishman
Who had more sense, who refused the cricket club,
The unspeakable in pursuit of the edible,
Because it made one assume such obscene positions.

Nocturne

Those other dreams, out of a former life,
Seemed to swarm at her ears as broken chords,
As music visible, a heightened world
Singing to the heart in exile—arpeggios
Lingering a little in the darkened air,
The minor calm, the dazzle, the return,
In arabesques, airy and unassailable.
Her past was living—"while, through the open window,
These cooling breezes, almost imperceptibly,
In caressing coils, in fitful eddies,
Were beginning their gentle nocturnes," Billie had played
Over and over the waltzes at Besançon,
Thought she could live forever in the fading bell
Of the tender, sad, exuberance of farewell.

Burton in Pieces

Ripple Effect

"I've given up drinking," my old teacher laughed,
Filling a water glass with burgundy.
Adding, "It's only wine," he drained off half
With the wry profundity of an epitaph.

Wet Work

"Do you think his thinking would change if he ever stopped?"
"Probably not. He's drinking with all he's got."

Addressee Unknown

He never replies. Very faithfully,
He guards old friendships in pure fantasy.

The Teacher in His Twenty-seventh Year

The autumn thorns toughen in the dry earth,
Ready to make their journey everlasting.
I catch one in my bike tire riding to school.
What have I brought with me that needs broadcasting?

The Regret of Heraclitus

after J. L. Borges's version of Camerarius

I who was many men will never rise
Once from the banks of Sophia Loren's thighs.

Of the Spheres

Sun-turning flowers, yellow on Thursday, bluejeans
On Monday, purple on your fingernail,
The grave chromatics of mismatched desire—
Billie had felt divided all her life.
Now—"Did you sigh? did you sigh?"—Billie could hear
Descending minor scales, the colorations
Of a universe of sound. As a little girl,
Singing with her girlfriends while they picked
Berries, cherries, raspberries, red currants,
She sang to keep from eating the bright red notes
Bending the trees and bushes. Now, as she stirred
The world within began to stir. All day
She played her records endlessly; all night
She watched those incandescent textures turning.

Burton in Heaven

"The world shall end like a comedy, and we
Shall meet at last in heaven." Glorious Gainsborough
Believed we would all heartily converge out here,
The lovely clouds and shaggy parks our home,
Constable, Monet, Rousseau, Ryder and Dove,
"And Van Dyke shall be of the company," and Beethoven
Hearing the wonders of his life, and Wilde
Dying beyond his means, sharp to the end,
"Either the wallpaper goes or I go,"
And Voltaire telling the priest when finally pressed
To renounce Satan and all his works, "this is
No time to be making new enemies," Rabelais
"Going to seek a great *perhaps*, they have
Already greased my boots." What jolly friends,
After the tears, the wringing hands, the last words,
For an endless end to melancholy: James
Madison, "I always talk better lying down,"
And Stonewall Jackson leaving as a Southerner
With an old soldier's communal sense and need,
"Let us cross the river and rest in the shade,"
And Hegel dialectical right to the end,
"Only one man ever understood me
And he didn't understand me either." Now we all
In one gigantic *castrum* will understand,

Not knowledge simply, but simply love of knowledge.
"The first step toward philosophy is incredulity"—
Even Diderot himself would never believe,
From this *"Cento* of all ages . . . one handsome Venus,"
That they couldn't recall whatever had left them behind.

Burton at Yoga

They had the heaters on in summer. Sweat
Made my feet slip on the tacky mat. Bikram
Began in Calcutta, the leader smiled, so the heat
Gives us a sense of origin. Why not dead
Bodies piled in the doorways, and legless beggars
Pleading with ladies dressed in pink, as rich
As Vishnu himself? I wondered. Yoga humor
Was not part of the package, but revenge
Fell swiftly, while I panted through each contortion,
Trying to ignore the aficionados, rapt
In poses out of a solo *Kama Sutra*. At the blessed end
The leader even corrected my corpse position.
I guess there's something nearly gratifying
About not getting that one quite right just yet.

Narcissus at Ninety

"He grasps the nettle as himself."

Odd, when the world is you, you can have enemies—
The world's your enemy, and you fear the world.
Solace, alone, comes from exploding gases
Of the star at the center of your imagings.
You watch, entranced, the glory of the fires,
Slow motion vortices of silent time
That have sustained you nearly a hundred years,
And will for another hundred if you have,
As you have always had, your only way.
Moons, families, constellations—the vast
Universe without you is a pool
Reflecting your secret fears, murmuring fragments
Of your own speech that you are mortal too,
Excrement the universe revolves around,
No more exorbitant than the despised masses
Whose star collapsed a thousand lifetimes back.

Around

He came to hear his life as she would hear it,
Then through the eyes and ears around the room,
A circle she had gradually drawn him to.
They were the world for him, and they made him real,
A trembling world, a trembling reality,
Starting to tell what happened to each other,
Their shame expanding to the brink of hope,
Well, almost, on a good day. Humility
Was here, a sphere they could feel turning,
Bearing them onward with a silent noise,
A rushing, whispering music, *here*. But *there*
Was another matter, for another day.
"Well, I'm all right, right now," was all he'd say.
When Yvonne summoned the group, "Round up all
The usual suspects," Billy whispered, "Me too."

La Salamandre

for Yves Bonnefoy

"The alcohol of the declining day
Will spill out on the stones," and there he is,
Burning and cool a moment, and then gone,
Product and agent of decomposition,
The solvent of our care. He has gone through hell,
Or at least another dim quotidian sun
Where formerly there were fires, and heraldry.
He dreams of quick clear water over stones,
Which never seems enough, and of pure air,
Of transformations in the purple light
Into wherever he is. A little alembic,
He would distill an essence of himself,
So lost, so fragile, so much everything
As to be nothing in the afternoon.

In Another Country

Why Billy waited no one ever knew . . .
He waited before breathing, answering the phone,
Writing a letter, going out the door,
Smoking his cigarettes down to the fingernail,
Nervy and catatonic. Fearfully
He waited for his father to come down the hall
"To have a little talk," hearing the rattle
Of the buckle as the belt snaked through the loops,
And then the long humiliating talks.
The Longhorn would make him cry, would make him promise
Never to do whatever he did again,
"Don't make your mother cry," but Billy knew
Who made her cry (she was crying in the next room now),
But he couldn't say it. Then they'd shake hands,
The little boy hopeful, heading for freedom, when
(Just as I touch the doorknob) the cold smile,
"We've got a little something to do." And they both knew,
No matter how far from that room he went in his head,
That the rattler would raise thick clotted screams from him,
My arms pinned between the bed and the wall,
With shame, like murder, flooding the neighborhood.

From the Highest Tower

Gravid with text, he leans into the room,
Shyest of pedants, never meets an eye.
He smiles and slowly nods toward the empty chair.
He has been drinking toward this for a lifetime,
His punchlines always in a foreign tongue,
With even a private tone for footnotes.   Thus,
Difficile est saturam non scribere,
Où est ma salle de déclamation?
Or *mon semblable, mon frère.* Flying over,
The missing man formation. A flag snaps,
A bugle glows, his acolyte becomes
Flesh almost and tabled at his tits,
As Crashaw said. At the drop of a pin
The planes are gone, the flag still, the bugle dark,
The phantom listener, the phantom man. The room.

Opening Line

"Was the universe a quotation?" Burton wondered—
"Thus is man that great Amphibian.
Either someone like us night-foundered here
(This pendant world, in bigness as a star
Of smallest magnitude close by the moon)
Groping for trouts in a peculiar river,
Or in the emptier waste, resembling air,
Servile to all the skyey influences.
Rejoice; for I will through the wave, and foam,
And shall in sad lone ways, a lively sprite,
Make my dark heavy poem light, and light,
'I am no pickpurse of another's wit.'
For who can speak of eternity without
A solecism, or think of it without an ecstasy?
For though through many straits, and lands I roam,
I launch at paradise, and I sail towards home.
Love me, that I may die the gentler way,
Tomorrow is just another name for today."

The Voice of the Oracle

"The climate's delicate, the air most sweet,
Fertile the isle, the temple much surpassing
The common praise it bears."

                         "I shall report,
For most it caught me, the celestial habits
(Methinks I so should term them) and the reverence
How ceremonious, solemn, and unearthly
It was i' th' off'ring!"

                     "But of all, the burst
And the ear-deaf'ning voice o' th' oracle,
Kin to Jove's thunder, so surprised my sense,
That I was nothing."

                       This is a winter's tale,

The Hinge

These visions of my death, my comings back,
The Billies, Burtons, secret, schizophrenic,
These fearful suspects of my dormancy,
The black stars doubling everything I saw.
The surviving twin and premature, I was
At four pounds thought too little to mutilate,
So my circumcision came when I was five,
A tonsillectomy thrown in. I was
Scared I am sure and mad—I must have been,
After all it had worked fine up until then,
And I saw no reason to make it shorter. But,
What I remember vividly was the ether,
The mask, the backwards counting, as I breathed,
I said, "I like this, it tastes like bubblegum."
Then I was nothing indeed. The next morning
My throat, to say nothing else, was too sore to eat
The ice cream I'd been promised. The nurse told me
"I've seen a lot of little boys dragged in here
For this business, but nobody, not a one of them
Ever said he loved the ether." I know now
If anyone ever gives you a drug
And you wake up in pain and they've cut off
The end of your dick and you think it was a good trip,
You've got a drug problem. Now I admit it,
I read as a boy of Dali, himself a boy,
Sitting in a public stall fervently

Repelled by a piece of mucus on the wall,
Until he wrapped some paper around his hand,
And wiped it off in holy terror. Dried solid,
It sliced his finger to the bone.
I have not told this story more than three times
In thirty-five years. There have been many others
At every door crying their secrecy,
I have not shaken them. Now as the sun returns,
I let these stories in and let them out,
Suzuki Roshi's door blowing in the wind
Open and shut, the spirit where it listeth,
The breathy constellations overhead
Turning the season. This was a winter's tale.

More Tender, and
Everywhere Open

Burton's been reading all day long. The world
Rolls from his eyeballs, a small distant globe
Whereon, in a little village in Périgord,
Five hundred years ago, in another tongue,
A father taught the villagers, for his son,
Latin, a few words still surviving. Majestically
The boy grew into the tongues of experience,
The demotic genius of his countrymen.
Burton dog-eared this book from the tribes of Gaul,
And the painters who dreamed their animals underground,
And Josephine Baker's chateau: "He deserves the whip
Who spends his time with wine and sauces." To this
Even royalty concurred—the Count with "splank,"
The Duke with irresistable defining swang.

Before Sleep

The Magdalene with the Smoking Flame
BY GEORGES DE LA TOUR

This room goes on forever. The dark hush
Glows like departing love that will not go.
There are no edges; here everything is rounded
By light and its companion. As if dazed,
She stares beyond the mortifying rope,
Even beyond the radiant candle flame
Deepening the room she sits in. Rising up
Out of the purifying light, a thread,
A smoky thin reminder, whispers that guilt
Is the mortal trail of spirit, arguing:
No light without shadow . . . flame without matter's ash.
She holds her contemplation like a breath,
Absently fingering a burnished skull
That answers only a little of her glow.

Poetic

with a line from Basil Bunting

"It might be from a handbook on recorders."

For one thing, it's on the air, you can hear music,
Knowing inflected by the ear. Not *wood*,
Not even *mouthpiece*, but the lovely *fipple*
("Hey, that's like nipple," my little daughter laughs),
And the conveyer of this joy's a player,
Whose breathing tunes the hollow that she fills,
Empties and fills again. I am caught up
In the roll of the hull, this ecstasy of naming,
This gathering up of more than fifty years
In a wide harbor, a life made up of words,
All of them here before we finally heard them,
And consolation rolling upon the tide:
As the player's breath warms the fipple the tone clears.
Ardor, attend us as our stars descend.